A Teenage Boy

Kaiden Sebastien

 FriesenPress

Suite 300 - 990 Fort St
Victoria, BC, V8V 3K2
Canada

www.friesenpress.com

ISBN
978-1-5255-6838-1 (Hardcover)
978-1-5255-6839-8 (Paperback)
978-1-5255-6840-4 (eBook)

1. YOUNG ADULT NONFICTION, SOCIAL TOPICS

Distributed to the trade by The Ingram Book Company

table of contents

"our" generation

we learn that the world is both beauty and bullshit,
that we are not adults but we cannot be children
the "grown ups" tell us what to do
and choose the future for us

but why don't i get to enjoy my time now?
i'm just a kid!

we're a special kind of crazy,
the "blow shit up" kind of crazy,
the "razor blades have two meanings" kind of crazy,
the "let's make a difference before we die (soon)" kind of crazy

self destructive impulses boil in the face of authority
what if we ran away?
what if we had sex?
what if we ran for office?
what if we stabbed someone?
curiosity kills us
faster than the doctors can
(figure out what the fuck is going on)

nobody knows what the future holds
that is,
nobody knows what we can do (yet)

put us to work,
hear us yell
destroy our *only* planet,
watch us fight,
and chop down our family trees because
this isn't their orchard anymore

garbage fills the streets of this sideways city
and the church is angry because we said love doesn't
have walls,
that self expression is actually a real *fucking* concept
if we had gotten along in the first place, there wouldn't be sides
now would there?
but no, you dehumanize us
out of fear of being overtaken
now how *grown up* is that?

what a rat race!
we turn on each other so quickly
you would think we were never friends
we can't vote for change yet
but we can conceive another helpless soul
so what is it?
what value do us teenagers hold?
how can we show you?

free kick

by the age of 20 society says you need to get your act together,
you need a job or you need to be in school to get a job
society needs glasses,
there are so many shades of grey in every situation,
life becomes a blur of black and white
but society sees numbers,
they see the age, income, cheques, receipts,
they hold onto them,
pin them to your back,
make them into conversation topics at dinner,

if age = x and your payday = y, then...
forget it,

what i'm trying to say is,
your age isn't as important as you think,
people age differently and people do differently,
if we didn't then we wouldn't be people
by the age of 20 the only thing you need to have accomplished
is becoming 20
don't let other people's lives become your goals.

graffiti

you might be in a house
that you do not own,
that you do not dictate
that you cannot control.

there are words that we cannot say,
and things we are not allowed to understand.

home,

family,

jobs,

interviews,

laws,

clubs,

school,

commitment,

relatives,

rules,

we all belong to a cesspool of organization
and when we act like we can fix it,
they "fix" us. street artists go to jail
when they were just trying to say
i want to feel alive again.
creative minds are labelled as insane,
maybe because there's something common between the two.

when you go to school you'll hear
   the bell doesn't dismiss you, i do.
ok boomer,
whatever gets your rocks off.
we aren't here to argue,
we're just here to "learn."

however, there *is* something we can do;
we can speak,
and say whatever we want,
nobody can steal the words from your mouth.

nobody gets to see your thoughts,
and nobody can crash your brainwaves

you have a lot more than you think,
and before you disagree, ask yourself;

      can you breathe?
       can you think?
       does your heart beat?

look at how much **power** you hold,
and you aren't even trying yet!

imagine what you can make
with this much **control**.

page 44

feel how cold <

Arthur's grand-daughter is eventually
killed, and *Arthur* becomes more
emotional than practical.
       "Last Stand"
" the breath after laughter."
The sense of a threat kills me. Kills me!
[have you ever seen someone else's
work and immediately craved it?]
Who are artists but poor copycats?
You won't like being last, you know.
take it. Take my life, i am craving death.
Write poetry books. If you don't want a
job, be a writer. If you want your job
to include suicidal thoughts everyday, become
a writer. If when you shout, nobody hears
you, become a writer.
   Puck -   I saw your mark already.
               It was very good!

patience

what a strange feeling,
to wish that you were the creator of everything you loved
to know that no matter what you buried
it would still be there the next day

                              how unrealistic,
             waiting for somebody else to come back to you
                              all the while knowing
                        that it will never happen

through the fence

in the midst of heavy winter
time stands still
the world sleeps,
and lives deaden down

life has pressed pause,
yet in the midst of a morning
i awoke with a purpose to explore
despite the ivory blanket around my home

clad in nylon, armed with shovel,
i thrust open the door to adventure
and when i reached the edge of my domain
i explored the ground beneath alabaster
imploring with a silver blade
queries of the handler

i did exactly as i had intended
when a voice from beyond me
ignited a crackling, monarch fire
thawing my frozen hands and then,
while it wasn't their season
i could hear the birds start singing again

selfish

don't worry,

give me enough time and i'll mess things up

i'm used to it by now,

i've become a self-fulfilling prophecy

when i was younger i didn't believe in love,

now all i believe in is heartbreak

i'm the one who caused it,

and i'm the only one who's still suffering

but that doesn't matter to you,

you've got enough to yourself, right?

everything you ever wanted is at your fingertips,

but you wouldn't hold me despite being that close.

scorched

first intertwined, a bonfire of passion
flaming hearts & sparking knives
a ferocity unkept, the wilderness of a primal beast
eyes opened to a universe of connection,

then flames had grown tame
what sparks once flew now fluttering
searching for where the heat was
where winter was dead and water moved to steam,
yes, it was a dream,
but only a dream to wake up and forget
nothing worth keeping beyond sleep,

and now
it is cold,
bodies crave the embers of what they had,
and they would do anything to keep from going numb
it took a bed and a look to feel again
but without, they became a shadow of their own flame
unable to keep what was once made natural
in the end it wasn't enough to keep them warm.

and in my dreams, we sang

not much of a singer, but i'll try to make it through,

too much of a dreamer, and all i dream is you,

i've been stuck in circles, don't know what i should do,

because i've always been dreaming, but just dreaming of you.

again

here i am again
stuck inside my bedroom
doesn't matter what i did today
always back inside my bedroom,

i'll replay those old songs we used to sing
i'll replay the records we'd been missing
i'll cover up my face and drown in tears
because all i ever wanted was you here,

it's been a long while
since you've graced my eyes
but every single day you ruin
cutting up my mind,

every time i breathe,
i know it's not for me
every time i want,
it's only you i need.

sexting after a party at 3:22am

i love u
[3:22am]

> no u don't
> [3:23am]

when i see u,
my heart rests
[3:25am]

> lying doesnt make
> anyone happy
> [3:28am]

u r just as valuable
as the rest of us
[3:28am]

> idk what inspires
> you to say that
> [3:29am]

when u broke yr mother's heart,
she forgave u that night
[3:30am]

> r u drunk?
> do u need a ride home
> [3:32am]

no, my son
i am far past dead
[5:21am]

the five stages of death

would it kill you
to look me in the eyes
would it be too much
to be happy together
how much would it cost

please say you love me
even though i know it's not true
tell me everything will be okay
before you kill me

a dream weaver
you will never be
i already know

if we reversed time
things wouldn't be any better

but you already knew that, didn't you?

fourteen reasons i deleted your number

One. because we haven't talked to each other
since high school

Two. i spent a lot of time
thinking about how much we did for each other
and came to the realisation
that if after all that we still moved on, then clearly
nothing lasts.

Three. because your brother still stars
in the local plays, and it's getting really annoying.
every time i see him i know he's *your* brother and
then i look at your number
and the call button taunts my fingers
in the way an ex might taunt your happiness

Four. my biggest fear is
that if i should hear your voice again,
it would return me to who i was
when we knew each other.
i can't afford to lose

all of this progress
even if it means cutting off the very people
that stood me up this high in the first place.
You were the first bricklayer

Five. because we saw each other at the grocery store
and you said "hey"
and i said "fine thanks"
and i think legally i'm not allowed to talk to you anymore
because of that

Six. ever since i was 16 years old the phone scared me.
i can only answer simple questions
but the people on the other end always ask me
what happened to my ankles
and i slam down the phone.
my mother always asks me why i answer
when no one is ringing and
i don't have the heart to tell her that i am afraid
i know it would break her heart.

Seven. because one morning in homeroom i was on your phone
and one of your apps had porn on it and i *know* i'd accidentally
bring that up if we ever talked again

Eight. what if i did call, and you were in Africa
and I could hear the screeching of children in the background
playing soccer
like we did at lunch hour
and you would tell me that they needed one more player
and ask me if i was doing anything at the moment.
how could i refuse an escape with someone like you?

Nine. the girl down the road from your house had a crush
on you
at 12 years old, we used to run away from her every time she
was nearby
laughing like bandits escaping a bank robbery
i still see her around our hometown sometimes
i remember how wanted you were
i remember how jealous i was

Ten. because no matter what we said or did
we could never recreate the best moments of our lives
even if it was us that made them

Eleven. i remember the shape of your doorway
how you had a mirror just before it in the hall
and you looked so much more like your mother than
your father.
how a hatchet made you feel like the biggest person in
the world
and your words never held the sting of regret

Twelve. you were the first person i ever told that i had seen
a ghost

Thirteen. we both admired the same girl in biology class
and we both admitted it to each other on the same day
in a stroke of generosity and self-loathing
i gave up, decided to be your wingman
you did all the work on your own and never needed help
i tried to help you regardless
and never contributed to your success, despite being under
that impression
i don't want to be told that i haven't changed
not by you

Fourteen. because you were my best friend.

partners

my life has always been an open book,
but the quill is starting to get heavy
i once had a co-author,
but after a terrible fight she left me

now i continue to write,
i've never felt so tired before
my eyes are far past white,
and i only want to write more

will my old partner ever read this?
i was hoping that she would
so she could see how i felt about her,
how she had made my world.

ode to pups

when i am at a low,
and have nowhere to go,
i think of stones
and my old home
where all my dogs still roam

little mouths a schnarfling,
teeny snoots a shmuffling,
blackish, brownish, blondish coats,
deserve many a ruffling

fluffy fur so perfect,
make me forget my purpose
paws and claws put the world at odds
and let me pause the circus.

how could it be?

your eyes are a fever,
your arms are a medical file
a bar code,
a bad night
i cannot wait
to be your lip balm

they want to hide them,
i want to heal them,
hidden scars are still scars, after all.

family

orbs of light,
wishes,
they fall as snow into dead
hay-filled fields
i am in a school building
filled with empty tables,
a building made of hollow rooms.
how strange that youth passes,
shorter than wood
shorter than skin
i breathe to tell the air i am here,
that i still exist

i am living in a world that has ended.

nothing is born here, and nothing will die
in this world, i am an oddity
to be the only one here is cold,
it is lonely

i am living in a world that has ended.

art class

oh my porcelain girl,
my true ceramic beauty
when will you break again?

i don't want to cut myself
on all of your pieces,

but i will
if i have to
again.

empty lighter

the worst part of sadness,
is that people cover their face when they cry
why would you cover up such   beauty?
the beauty of   fracture,
the beauty of   things   falling   apart.

in case of emergency

it was at the kitchen sink
at 4:28am
when i was throwing up white powder and crying
that i realized there might be something wrong with me

this evil white powder fled swiftly
even the inanimate cannot resist the urge to abandon me
the universe scooped it out of my throat
saying *not now, malignant child.*

this powder
contained in adorable little green and white capsules
feigned help for any poor soul who dared take one pill at a time
i knew better than to listen to directions
but even i could only manage to cough my regret down
the drain
before falling to the floor at the bottom of the house

yes this, this is where my story starts
where it - really – starts
on the tiles of a dimly lit kitchen
empty lungs resonate with an empty heart.
a hollow shell of a boy
stays down on the ground after i stand up
i think he is still there, but i cannot summon the strength
to look
for fear of finding out.

for the past few years,
i took to walking aimlessly down narrow streets
where you can still hear the knuckles of the city *crack*
no map, no compass
time, and sound.
i was once human!
i would call out to the starry night
the sonic sinkhole that is a barren alleyway
there would be no answer, of course
no remorse for just another wandering soul
no god will give us direction,
it is against the rules to know what will happen next.

for days after lying on that kitchen tile
my throat burned bright cardinal
my spit was tainted with false hope
and i couldn't drink pop anymore.
my dad used to ask me why i kept glasses of it
out in my room for days on end

but who was i to tell him
that it was so the pill bottle on my bedside table had a friend?

together, they were my rainy day fund
a self-destruct button prescribed with good intentions
i swore to the doctor *yes, i will listen to the label*
but i think even he knew this would happen.

there's a special kind of shame that comes with a failed
suicide attempt.
people look at you differently, whether or not they know
what happened
the world is just a little more fucked up than before
and everybody seems a bit too kind.

you'll die anyways, why not wait? they say
as they skip ads on Youtube
you're going to be alright, they say
as if alright is all i ever wanted to be

i am locked in a box of perfection,
and it is a box in which I can *not* fit

i am the culmination of everything you wish
you said to me before it was too late

yes i… am tired

i was tired and those pills were a bed
and i broke open the covers and drowned them
and for 23 minutes (yes, i timed it)
i was the most content i had ever been.

please

at my funeral
please have two caskets
she will join me in time, if there is still room

and please,
don't cry
this was going to happen anyways

at my funeral
please let me hold a bouquet of yellow roses
i want to give them to her when she comes,

and please,
be happy that i am gone
for i am merely an integer

at my funeral
don't say my name
i don't want to scare her away again

and please,
won't you *please* cremate me
so my ashes may be free to explore the universe once and
for all.

faces

call me michael myers,
because i want to stab you

call me james bond,
because i want us to have sex way too early
and i too, fear that any day could be my last
call me anytime,
i know you won't
you have better people to call,
to call your own

call me a nightmare,
because it was a long and terrifying night, but i'm gone now
you woke up and thought you were better,
and that was the last time you slept in my bed

call me a murder-suicide,
because you killed my heart
and i killed my own inhibitions
i know there's blood on your hands,
but all i have left to give is salt

call me a phoenix,
because when you burnt me down to ashes,
i rose.

confetti from the horse's mouth

i have a problem.

it's 1pm and you're in my head

do i get out of bed?

we never slept but,

you gave me rest all the same.

i'm here because you're out there,

and maybe that's selfish,

maybe you were selfish,

but you don't care.

i have a problem.

now it's 5pm and i see your head

do i want to approach her?

we always talked but,

i never knew you were the same.

i go because she has your smile,

and it's just for empty sex,

on cluttered empty beds,

but i don't care.

because i have a problem.

it's 9pm and we're at her place

do i want to be here?

we always met but,

i never was quite the same.

i'm here because she shares your name,

and that could be coincidence,

maybe you set up this instance,

but i know you don't care.

i have a problem.

now it's 1am and i'm in her bed

do i care about her?

we never touched but,

i feel you all the same.

i'm here because she has your hair,

and maybe that's selfish,

maybe i am selfish,

but i don't care.

gaia

there will never be a happy ending when all remain unaware,
there will never be peace when we remain at arms with the
very ground we walk upon
a parasite as large and vast as us will rot this earth into dust and
dry rock,
long as it deems fit for our own personal gain
draining forest and sea, flora and fauna,
stripping away nature in front of its mother's very eyes
we have written our own ending tragic and sorrowful,
and we will still complain about how it was written,
because although we have been warned countless times of
our fate,
we will never be convinced that we are in danger until,
when we leave this planet,
in hopes of polluting more celestial beings than we were
first graced,
only then will we be able to look back and understand the
damage we have caused
but before it is too late, we will never waver, we will never
stray our path from forgiveness,
until we are ashes, we will forever burn.

the first of your kind

i want to say i love you,
but as soon as i see you,
my throat closes shut,
my heart begins to sprint,
my hands open for you,
fresh as the first spring flower,
yearning for your warm embrace.

i want to say i love you,
every time you're in my sight,
every time i receive one of your texts,
every time i get to hear your beautiful voice,
singing gorgeous melodies for me,
and only me.

you make my ears bleed honey,
you reduce me to only my goodness
your tongue dances around my open flame,
as i shine ever brighter for you.

i want to say i love you,
because i so, so love you,
when we embrace,
i feel the weight of the world fly off of my shoulders,
and push us ever closer together,
attached at more than just the hip,
our puzzle-piece bodies fit together so well,
it has become impossible to imagine us apart anymore.

i want to say i love you,
because you are my last good thought before i sleep
every night,
because when i ask the celestial beings the question "why?"
you are always the answer,
because every time i ask myself "why aren't you gone yet?"
the only answer i have is because i don't want to hurt you.

i want to say i love you,
because i know for a fact,
that there is nobody else in this entire universe,
that could be as perfect for me as you,
and when fate brings us to the cosmos from where we
once came,
my only wish is that i may be with you when it happens.

i want to say i love you,
and i did,

i loved you.

crushed

it's hard to look at the sky
　　　　see that your goals are still up there
　　　　　　　　and all you have in your hand is a shovel
yeah, it's really hard to expect
　　　　the warm, glowing sunshine
　　　　　　　　to warm up a raincloud
but what am i to do
　　　　except keep loving you
　　　　　　　　you haven't done a thing and yet
　　　　　　　　　　　　i'll fall the way i never do.

because loving you,
　　　　is like trying to fly
　　　　　　　　with cinder blocks for shoes
　　　　yeah loving you
　　　　　　　　is trying to catch flies
　　　　　　　　　　　　with vinegar on your hands

　　　　because loving you
　　　　　　　　is the best and the worst thing
　　　　　　　　　　　　i couldn't ask for a more
　　　　　　　　　　　　pleasant torture.
　　　　so please,
snap my neck with your pinky fingers
　　　　your adorable little pinky fingers
the pinky fingers that are making me cry as i write this stupid
poem about you.

cut me deeply with your voice
        deeper than i ever could
               let my brain cook in your audio waves,
        more than i have cooked my entire life
if i'm going to die by your hand
        then you better give it your all.

write your name on my eyes
        in blood and tears of hopeful joy
               so i can always see you
                       even after you leave me like they
                       all do.

                              i really shouldn't be

like this,
for so long

                         i've been cold in the dirt,
                                no, this time

i really feel something,
this time

                    it's gonna really fucking hurt.

apocalypse for one

friendships only make this cold world turn blind,
when you cross me i won't be fine at all,
i'd rather become my own friend in mind
but if i love you i will take the fall.

mother earth is dying to father time,
and nobody seems to even take care
the only thing i can do is make rhyme,
there is only one girl for whom i care.

this life is impossible to lead on,
yet still i will continue all the same
when darkness comes for all i have begot
i won't give them a clue beside my name.

i wish to leave nothing special behind,
my dreams and memory of her in mind.

never enough
for daniel kyre

daniel kyre, daniel kyre,
now he was a man of grand desires
so funny and lovable and always so kind,
he never could leave a person behind
an avid film student and skilled guitarist,
a comic who always held his heart in his fist
he hungered for fame, starting a youtube channel,
it was the start of a golden age for daniel
he and his best colleague ryan magee,
started to make short films every few weeks
they caught the attention of a much larger fish,
and this fish was willing to grant them a wish

daniel kyre lit a fire,
and brandished with him big desires
his hometown was too slow for him,
and he had bigger films to film
so he got his friend ryan and they packed their bags,
and they travelled to the city of riches and rags
"los angeles, ho!" the two men hollered,
as the buildings around them grew taller and taller
they got an apartment and perfected their art,
they were so much bigger than they were at the start
his father then texted him, always so sappy,
he ended his last text with *"well, are you happy?"*

but he wasn't.

he wasn't happy on the inside
he wanted to be a star.
demons flooded his mind
and he held the dam
until the moment he drowned.
an infected brain makes a victim
and the body is just the evidence
it will always result in tragedy
a mouthful of pills.
daniel kyre was ill
and he never told anyone
he wanted to make people laugh
and laughing people don't talk about sadness
happy people only talk about how to stay happy
success only wants more success
and maybe that was the death of a young star
a constellation of creation can only shine so bright
daniel was doing exactly what he had wanted
but mental illness is not a kind god
and he became a sacrifice of nobody's will.

baby's first heartbreak

i hold my heart in two pieces, cram them together,
when it isn't fixed i cry
i cry and cry and cry,
that someone else can put them together
and when i see another hand,
i'm so very happy
i have someone to fix me,
as if that's not my responsibility
i cling to the helpful arm,
render it useless until
they finally fix the heart,
and i promise to never lose it
i play with it all i want,

> i throw it and i laugh
> then i fumble on the heartstrings,
> and it breaks with a crash
> now here we are again,
> the hand has long been gone
> i guess i'll have to wait,
> until another comes along.

to know too much

i wish   i was stupid,
i wish   i didn't know the names of the seven seas,
i wish   i didn't know how much
i lost   when i lost you.

poison

masculinity,
mirror.

reflective,
fragile.

unnecessary,
obsolete.

don't you miss me?

i don't get it
it was broken before he got there
he opened the door to a chair
and a bad dream come true

she had a lot to live for
and he hurt everyday for her
he already had
but pain could never hope to stop time

the days ran over him
a stampede
don't open your mouth

they know she did this for a reason
but how dare they ask
maybe next time somebody rests
they can start to ask questions

don't you miss me too?

you don't get it

it was broken before I got there

I opened the door to a Chair and a bad Dream come true

She had a lot of memories in progress

and I suffer everyday on Her behalf

but pain doesn't make Time stop

the days,

they run over me

a stampede of Her steel-toed boots

don't open your mouth if you want to keep your teeth!

we know She did this for a reason

but how *dare* we ask

maybe next time somebody rests we can ask questions again

we are still wishing

sometime someday i said i skipped school on a whim,
she said she had skipped school on a whim similarly
such a wild coincidence,
a *cowhimcidence,* if you will.

what a weird starry word,
such a weird starry world
she says she's started to wilt with the wilderness,
i wonder why someone would want that.

what a wonder,
what a wonderful world with her
when we wilt,
i wonder what we will want.

where will she walk,
i wonder if i will walk with her
when we waver apart,
i wonder whether we will still stay a wish.

participation award

I have an overactive mind

I can visualize a clone of myself
hanging in my own closet
with all of our sweaters and jackets

i can see a world where you aren't mad at me,
a world without white waters
rain without the clouds
wind without bright lightning

but i can only see it
and there are many steps between seeing
and being

because being
is more than seeing
and far beyond believing,

the world has every wrinkle flattened out.

all lapels are folded
every inch of print is typed
this book is filled
and we are in it, until we are written out

when i was 10 years old
i knew that i was going to die
i had no clue how or when
but i knew it would be on purpose
something no mother wants to hear

but my mother did,
and she got me a therapist named sherry
and sherry was great,
several years after,
i would see her at the grocery store and i would thank her for
saving my life,
but only inside my head.
there is a lot that should be said,
that ends up staying inside instead

after a few months, i stopped seeing sherry
i was convinced that the cold on my cheeks without wind was
just how the world felt

that if you weren't hurting then maybe there was just some-
thing wrong with you, that when you did something wrong and
got punished for it you were never forgiven.

it started again in high school. I became a bomb with an invis-
ible fuse.
Nobody knew when I would blow,
i learned how much distance you could earn when you make
people fear the sound of a ticker
i would keep my fingers on the clicker,
"dont come too close or I'll pull the trigger!"

A Teenage Boy

then i started seeing mary,
and mary was great
she said i had all these pieces, i just needed to put them
in place,
you see mary wasn't like sherry,
she had her own problems she buried
but in her office she had a pair of shovels
every appointment we'd sort through the rubble
for an expedition of ours
to see how deep we could dig in an hour
and although sometimes it was rough
it helped us uncover the sweet and the sour

but then i graduated
from all of the awful classes i hated
the moment that we had all anticipated
was here, and now we had no idea what to do
at least, I know I didn't have a clue

so i took to the papers in my room,
and i decorated them in black and blue,
my body may rot, but my ink lasts forever
so while my mind vomits onto paper
i can at least pretend i wont be fully gone

when i become a clone of myself,
and i hang in my closet with our sweaters and jackets

you can at least remember that i tried

cold

it's winter in my mind
and i know that sounds sublime
but there's snow, such terrible night
so much aching in my mind
the only thing i have is time
i don't dream when i close my eyes
and if you asked me, I'd be fine
But we all know and we all lie

yes it's winter in my mind
and i know that sounds subliminal
yet i act just like a criminal
when my brainwaves hit their minimal
i can see only the critical
moments passing lineal
make my life cynical
knowing far past your pinnacle

it's winter in my mind
and i know that sounds insane
but the snow inside is grey
and i know that's not so great
i show the public world my pain
because i know it's the only way
to make you feel the same.

my only love is a sickle

i am an imitator,
a mimic of a child reaching out for the toy taken from their
loose grasp,
only wanting things once they are gone,
i become what i hate simply because,
i am that which i hate,

though infancy may remain inside,
my mind has already grown so old,
i feel my death every moment,
i see the sickle around my neck,
everyday leaning into it a hair more,

the smells of a graveyard linger,
calling my name in full,
my companion's laughter may only echo,
filling the empty chambers of my heart,
and where once i was full,

yes i have giants left to slay,
and maybe a colour or two left to find,
lands to roam and seas to swim,
but i am just fine stopping here,
as continuing alone is what i fear most

Kaiden Sebastien

fragments

sometimes,
some days,
i look at something or someone,
and i see a fragment.

a fragment of something i've always wanted,
a fragment of something i never wanted to lose,
a fragment of you.

the wonder of you,
is that you are all of the fragments put together
glued together with ivory skin,
stitched with my old clothes,
topped with soft and silky hair,
magnetic to my hands,
like your skin is a magnet to my lips.

if i could control time,
i would rewind to when we first saw each other
our first conversation,
our first date,
just before our first argument.

if only i had taken your advice,
and really fulfilled what i should have,
i could have saved us,
i could have saved myself.

i wish i had the same effect on you,
that i wasn't worthless
i hope you tell me you love me again,
before i break into fragments of my own.

> "it's been a few years since you've been gone,
> there's been a few tears but that was years and years ago,
> yeah i grew up to be exactly what you wanted,
> yeah i've been living out the dream that you dreamt up,"
> **"crash"**
> **jonathan ng**

not my future

when you were thirteen years old
you showed me a poem,
and i loved it,
the way you waxed poetic,
though you were so young,
you knew what a piece depended on,
every word as important,
as how you made me feel,
any moment with you never a moment too long,
it's been a few years since you've been gone,

i remember it clearly,
you hugged a noose as if it was your only friend
yeah, it was *that* sudden
nobody else saw the battlefields in your irises
and with such a quiet voice,
nobody ever had the chance to know
the grace of a girl wiser than time
i finally found out when it was already too late,
when your mother screamed at me over the phone
there's been a few tears but that was years and years ago
i've never forgotten your voice
and you star in my fevered dreams,
when everyone is too much to bear
i tolerate only your gentle chords,
you were such a celestial writer
but your galaxy so suddenly stunted,
now i have picked up the pen and paper
and begun where you had left off,
i feel as though my life is truly haunted
yeah i grew up to be exactly what you wanted,
even now,
i understand my calling,
writing so fluid and natural
i've thought of my own ideas,
i'm no longer the robot of society's invention
and this craft is not just feverish burn up,
everyday i'm writing i wish you were here
and i know that this is where you have been,
you were winter's brightest young buttercup
yeah i've been living out the dream that you dreamt up,

family traditions

my father told me this when i was young,
that if you wanted to get over something you just had to get it
over with,
rip off the bandage and face the cut
because if you just ignored it the pain would build,
higher and higher, bigger and bigger
if you control the pain you can overcome it,
you'll thank yourself later
he said
so sincerely i was convinced he knew what he was
talking about

i remember still, at 10 years old,
i agreed with it,
and anyone i didn't like was gone
i kept my therapist and my family
and even then at arms length,
men didn't feel pain back then,
or so i was told
and like magic,
everyone started to distance me,
just as i had done to them
i was taught then that it meant i was mature,
you'll thank yourself later
i would echo,
as i walked the empty halls full of peers.

my father told me this when i was young,
that in order to get over pain you had to rip off the bandage,
get it over with, make the cut,
if your friends are drifting just cut it,
if she isn't interested just cut it,
you'll thank yourself later.
the minute i sensed it,
i went to her house with her things,
and yeah, maybe i regret it more than anything,
but it would have hurt more if i stayed,
right?

i never saw my dad cry
i never sensed his emotional pain
i never heard him say
i love you,
and i certainly never felt it
so it was odd when i found out who he really was,
such a liar, i thought
he wasn't afraid to feel behind closed doors
no, instead he leaned on the backs of those doors
aching to show somebody that he needed help,
his throat full of thorns, he still remembered,
that his father before him, my grandfather,
always said,
you'll thank yourself later,
yet i did not see a grateful man before me.

let me

when i go,
feel my emptiness in your house
let me empty your heart,
and pour it into the ocean,
make your blood dissolve in salt.

when i go,
remember how much i meant to you,
or how much i never meant to you
let me inflict my presence on you,
a black hole of lost energy.

when i go,
dump your tears in the ocean,
where i have dissolved your blood
let me use my black hole,
and drain the water away.

when i go,
i will be gone nonetheless,
let me waste away to nothingness,
i want to achieve nothing less,
there should be nothing left.

scenes from a hotel lobby

1. a man sets a table for him and his two daughters. he spends the hour looking with a woven face at aged photographs while they eat.

2. three young boys ask for a night's stay in exchange for two coins and a candy wrapper. their demeanours wither when their offer is declined.

3. two lovers with matching dresses approach the desk to book a room for friday night.
   they giggle with glee at each step of the process.

4. a young woman dressed in all white asks if the building has rooftop access. she is disappointed with the clerk's answer and leaves shortly thereafter.

5. the mailman delivers a letter to an elderly couple in the lobby. they open the envelope together, softly. teardrops stain the loose-leaf.

6. a man in the lobby tells jokes and laughs loudly. his humour darkens with the sky.
   he asks the clerk why the world won't take no for an answer. the laughter stops.

growing pains

i hate black coffee,
the sourness and unforgiving taste,
the beans want you to know that this wasn't meant to be,
inside, you know your life was never supposed to be spent
on them
you're an adult,
they say,
these things are just what you have to deal with.
i hate working,
clocking in to work a job i hate,
going home for an evening of sighs and blinks,
just to go back again after another sleepless night
you're an adult,
they say,
these rules are just what you have to live by.
i hate living most days,
the fact that we are trapped in these boxes of buildings,
pretending we have control over what little we are allowed,
just to die and be replaced by the next faker in town
you're an adult,
they say,

but if this is what an adult is then kill me now.

clay

i am not but one human, as i wished
we are all connected

all of us are pieces of a broken bowl
one definitive template
the eyes, the limbs, the organs
they have all changed
the goals, the ideas, the cultures,
they have been transformed

i can only hope
i have made something unique,
something unlike any of us,
a difference.

when i return to the bowl,
when i change into another piece of clay,
i hope i may see my difference come with me.

our generation

so, how *can* we show them?

we may be Atlas,
but we have many shoulders
there may be a day zero,
but our hands are on the clock

they covered the sky like a smoke grenade,
and for the first time in history, we celebrate tear gas
this time, we're coming to *their* house,
and when we're gone, there won't be anything left to love

so take the books,
but leave those privileged quills to dry
ransack the valuables,
but leave the old values on the shelf

call us renegades, bandits, thugs, punks, whatever you want,
they're just fancy names for those who change history
and if you want to join us,

all you have to do is swallow what silicon pride you have left

this isn't a hate speech to our ancestors, no,
this is for the racist grandma's comments to the Native cashier,
for the father who just kicked their daughter from the closet to
the curb,
yeah, we're talking to *you*

this is call-out *culture* now,
nobody gets away scot-free
we're not about forgiveness if what you did is unforgivable
and don't get us *started* on apologies
saying sorry doesn't un-hit a child,
and it won't make your hands any lighter either
if the only thing you can offer is a sentiment,
then maybe you should stop admiring yourself in the mirror

we can all make it together, as crazy as it sounds
it's just gonna take a lot of effort (on both ends)
so when you're done reading this piece, let's get to work.

let's show the world what we can do.

acknowledgements

I would like to thank the editors and staff of FriesenPress for giving me the opportunity to tick a box on my bucket list; Marbles for always being there even when it felt like nobody else wanted to be; my mother Wasylyna for being just the best ever; my father Shane for being the much-needed voice of reason in my life; and finally,
Corey, Devon, Luc, Ty, Kieran, and Jax
for not *really* knowing what I was doing, but supporting it anyways.

And I would like to thank you for reading this. You are the most important part of all of this. And for that, I could never thank you enough.

credits

"not my future" Glosa excerpt from "crash" by Jonathan Ng [EDEN]

"never enough" devoted to Daniel Kyre (Rest in peace)

"family traditions" inspired by Phil Kaye's "Repitition"

"14 reasons i deleted your number" inspired by Doc Luben's

"14 Lines From Love Letters Or Suicide Notes"

author bio

Kaiden Sebastien is an undergraduate student at Vancouver Island University working toward a degree in creative writing. He has been writing short stories and poetry for over a decade and won awards for his writing in high school. He wishes he lived in a treehouse with a witch named Azure, baking fresh bread and dancing to old jazz vinyls, but for now he just lives in Ladysmith, BC.

CPSIA information can be obtained
at www.ICGtesting.com
Printed in the USA
LVHW091415011120
670390LV00024B/706

9 781525 568398